Chocolate!

Diana Noonan

Contents

A World of Chocolate

What is the best **invention** ever?
Is it the car?
Is it the computer?
Is it **chocolate**?

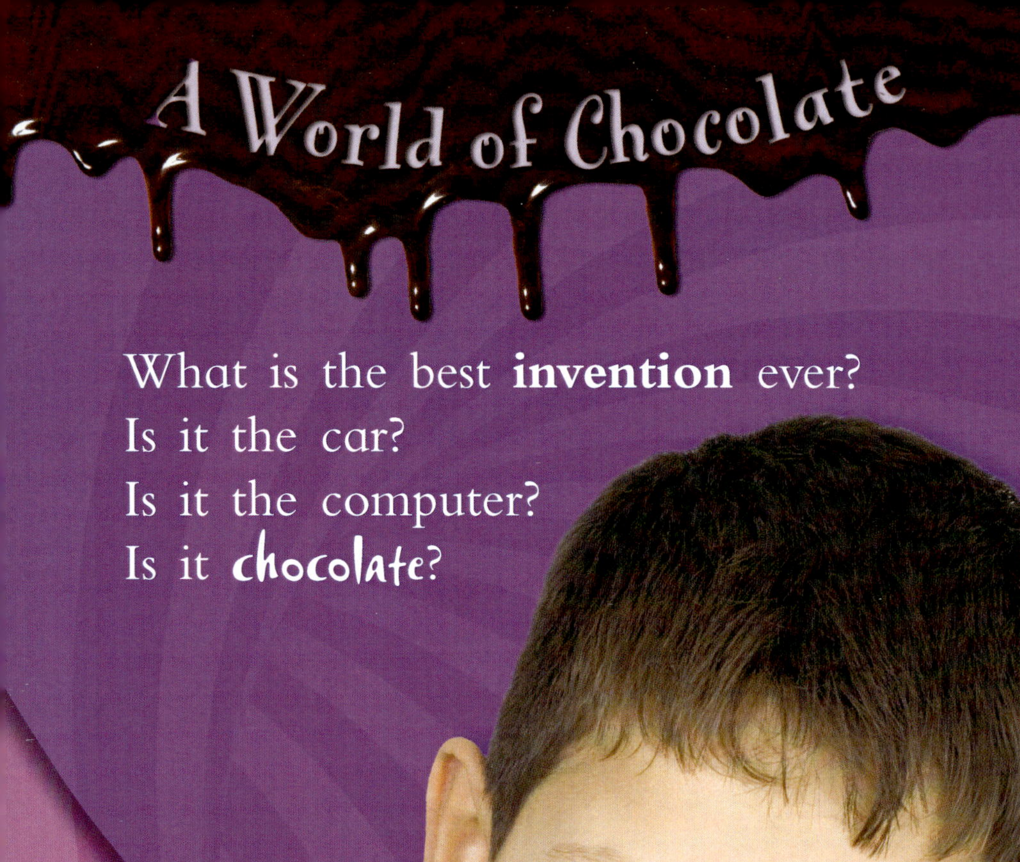

We eat chocolate.

We drink it.

We cook with it.

We give it as a gift.

Most of us love chocolate.

A Chocolate Tree?

Chocolate does not grow on trees. But chocolate is made from cocoa beans. Cocoa beans come from **cacao** trees.

Cocoa beans are seeds. They grow in **pods** on the cacao tree.

The pods grow on the trunk and branches of the cacao tree.

Workers pick the cocoa pods from the tree. They cut open the pods and take out the beans.

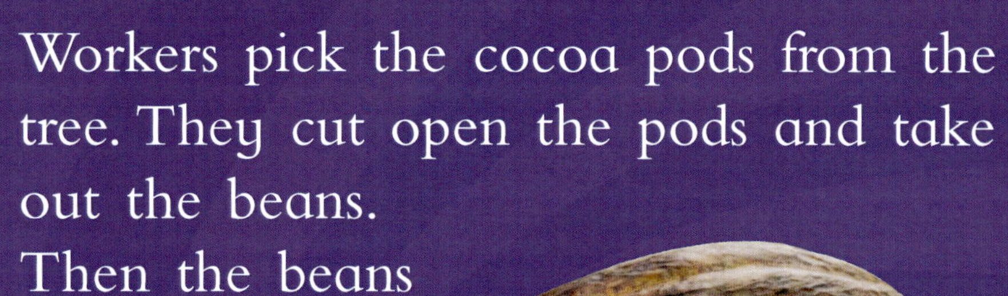

Then the beans dry in the sun.

After they are dry, the cocoa beans are put into bags. Ships take the bags all over the world. Trucks take the bags to chocolate **factories**.

In some countries, cacao farmers are very poor. When you buy Fairtrade chocolate, you know that the farmers have been paid fairly for their work.

A Famous Book about Chocolate

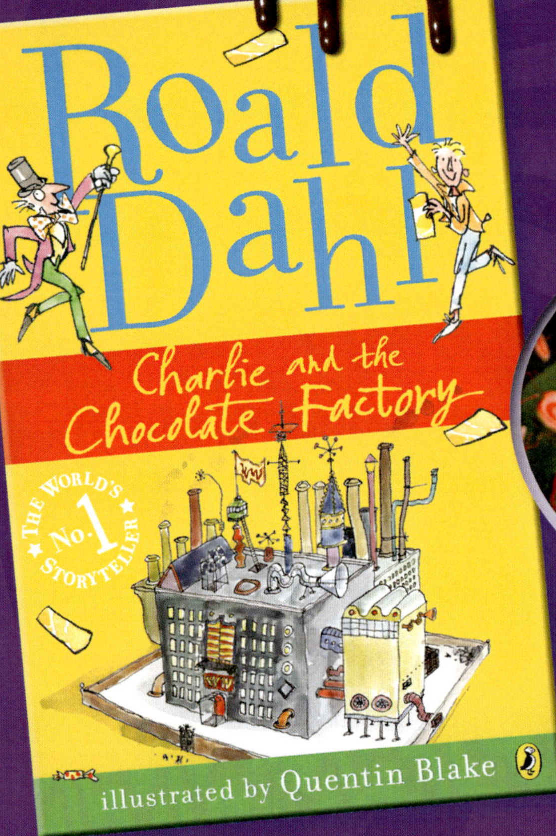

Films have also been made of *Charlie and the Chocolate Factory*.

Charlie and the Chocolate Factory is a very famous book. In the book, Charlie meets Willy Wonka. Willy Wonka owns a chocolate factory.

Willy Wonka keeps his chocolate **recipes** a secret. But **spies** from other chocolate factories try to steal them.

Secret Recipes

Real chocolate factories keep their recipes a secret, too. At one chocolate factory, a **machine** broke. A person came to fix the machine. He had to wear a blindfold as he walked in and out of the factory. This was to make sure he did not see any chocolate secrets!

You can visit chocolate factories. You can see how chocolate is made. You can even eat the chocolate. But the recipes are secret!

How Chocolate Is Made

This is what happens inside a chocolate factory. First, the cocoa beans are roasted.

Then, a machine crushes the roasted beans into bits. Their shells come off.

roasting the beans

shells come off

The broken cocoa bits are called nibs. The nibs are crushed into chocolate **paste**. The paste is used to make different kinds of chocolate.

chocolate paste

nibs

All Kinds of Chocolate

Cocoa is made from pressed and dried chocolate paste.

Cooking chocolate is made from cooled chocolate paste.

Dark chocolate is made from chocolate paste, cocoa butter and sugar.

Milk chocolate is made from chocolate paste, cocoa butter, sugar and milk.

Chocolate Takes Shape

There are many kinds of chocolate shapes and chocolate blocks.

This is a chocolate block. You may have eaten chocolate like this.

Chocolate is melted and tipped into special **moulds** to make shapes. Perhaps you have eaten a chocolate rabbit!

This rabbit is made of white chocolate.

Yum!

The chocolate is being poured into a mould.

Imagine drinking chocolate from a chocolate fountain. Look at all the runny chocolate.

Have you eaten chilli chocolate? Chocolate is yummy but chillies are hot! What would it be like to eat **spicy** chocolate?

There is also chocolate that has pepper in it.

The Chocolate Hall of Fame

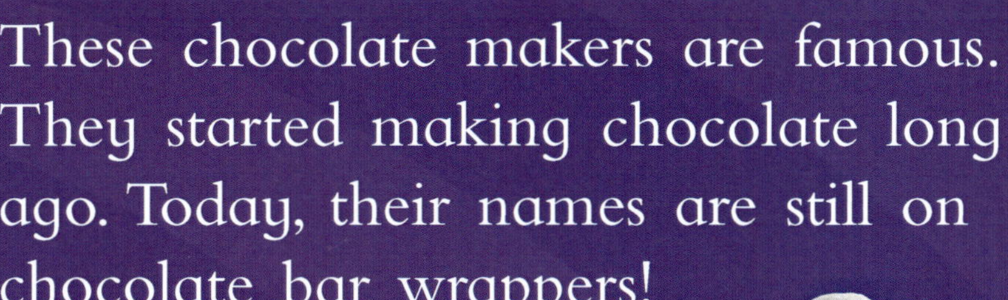

These chocolate makers are famous. They started making chocolate long ago. Today, their names are still on chocolate bar wrappers!

Rodolphe Lindt
(1855–1909, Switzerland)
Made extra-smooth chocolate

Milton Hershey
(1857–1945, USA)
Built a chocolate factory in 1905

Chocolate Bites

Every part of this pizza is made of chocolate, even the cheese!

Tasty Joke

Q: Why did the chocolate chip cookie go to the doctor?

A: Because it was feeling crummy.

The biggest chocolate egg ever made was 8 metres high. It weighed as much as a family car!

Chocolate Quiz

How much can you remember about chocolate?

1 Cocoa beans are:
 a chocolate beans
 b seeds
 c fruit

2 Dark chocolate is:
 a made with milk
 b made with dark-coloured cocoa beans
 c made without milk

3 Chocolate is shaped in:
 a moulds
 b tins
 c bottles

Chocolate Quiz Answers

1 b 2 c 3 a

Glossary

blindfold	material tied over your eyes
cacao	a small tree that grows in tropical areas
cocoa	dried and powdered chocolate paste
cooking chocolate	a chocolate with a stronger taste, used in baking
factories	buildings with equipment for making things
invention	a clever idea or discovery
machine	an object used by people to help them do work
moulds	hollow shapes made of plastic or metal
paste	a smooth, soft mixture
pods	a strong outer covering for seeds
recipes	directions for cooking something
spicy	with strong heat
spies	people who steal secret information